the guide to owning
Dwarf Rabbits

Dennis Kelsey-Wood

T.F.H. Publications, Inc.
One TFH Plaza
Third and Union Avenues
Neptune City, NJ 07753

ISBN 0-7938-2162-2

This book has been published with the intent to provide accurate and authoritative information in regard to the subject matter within. While every precaution has been taken in preparation of this book, the author and publisher expressly disclaim responsibility for any errors, omissions, or adverse effects arising from the use or application of the information contained herein. The techniques and suggestions are used at the reader's discretion and are not to be considered a substitute for veterinary care. If you suspect a medical problem, consult your veterinarian.

www.tfhpublications.com

Contents

Introduction

Rabbits have been kept by humans for so long that it is not even known for certain when or where domestication first took place. However, by pooling their specialty knowledge, archaeologists, zoologists, and historians have developed an acceptable theory.

Rabbits have been kept as domestic pets throughout history.

The wild species from which all domestic rabbits have been developed is *Oryctolagus cuniculus.* Its common name is the Old World, or European, rabbit. The original distribution range is thought to have been restricted to southern France and the Iberian peninsula (Spain and Portugal). It is quite possible that the rabbit was taken from Spain to North Africa via the Straits of Gibraltar during the Bronze Age.

The Phoenicians developed a large merchant shipping fleet that explored the whole of the Mediterranean and sailed into the Atlantic. It is thought that these people first took rabbits from Spain to Egypt and Asia Minor prior to 1,000 B.C. The early Romans were probably responsible for introducing the rabbit to northern European countries, while the Normans are credited with taking rabbits to Britain during the Fourth century.

Spanish, French, Dutch, and British colonists introduced the rabbit to countries throughout their empires, as well as to uninhabited oceanic islands. By these means, the European rabbit has become established in most countries in the world. It has been especially so where there were no native predators or other rabbit species to restrict the success of the introduced species.

Such introductions, intended to be beneficial to humans, have backfired and created enormous problems. On small islands, the rabbits denuded areas of vegetation that previously gave cover to ground nesting birds. In Australia, vast tracts of agricultural land were devastated. In an effort to rectify the error, humans merely compounded it by introducing ferrets and cats to countries where these animals were not native.

Unfortunately, these predators had a greater impact on the native mammals and birds than they did on the rabbits! Such are the problems when we attempt to tamper with nature, in which evolution has created an order of things that is delicately balanced.

SCIENTIFIC STANDING

For many years, the rabbit was classified as a rodent. But it was realized that rabbits had enough anatomical differences to warrant placing it and its close relatives in a separate major group, or order, as it is called by zoologists. The order is called Lagomorpha and contains hares, rabbits, and pikas (conies). There are 69 species in this order, of which 47 are hares and rabbits.

Rabbits are found in most parts of the world except for Australia, New Zealand, Madagascar, the West Indies, southern South America, and many small oceanic islands.

The distinction between a hare and a rabbit is sketchy. There are cranial differences, and, in general, hares are larger and have black tips to their ears. They live above ground, making crude nests, whereas rabbits dig burrows. Baby hares are born fully furred, with their eyes open, and can run around within minutes of birth. Rabbits are born blind, naked, deaf, and cannot move out of their burrow for some weeks. The terms rabbit and hare are often used incorrectly. The Belgian Hare is a domestic rabbit, while the Jack Rabbit and Snowshoe Rabbit are actually hares.

The most obvious feature that distinguishes a lagomorph from a rodent (order Rodentia) is that the paired incisors of the upper jaw are doubled—one tooth behind the other. Rodents have single-paired incisors. Lagomorphs also have either no tail (pikas) or very short ones (rabbits and hares). Rodents, with some exceptions, have long tails.

BREED DEVELOPMENT

The Romans kept rabbits and hares in large enclosures called *lepororii.* They did not conduct planned breeding but allowed nature to take its course.

However, during the Middle Ages, monks started to be more selective in the rabbits that they bred. In this way they could increase the size of rabbits produced. They also found that non-

Inbreeding for characteristics such as size and color developed the Dwarf Rabbits we see today.

Rabbit clubs were formed to discuss different breeds, color patterns, and types of rabbits. Netherland Dwarfs were identified as a breed in 1948.

wild colors started to appear in their stock and that these new colors could be passed on to other rabbits. The new colors were mutations, but at that time the science of genetics was unknown. Even so, it can be said that the development of breeds, and certainly breed types, originated in the monasteries and rabbitries of wealthy Europeans during the 16th century.

THE RABBIT FANCY BEGINS

One of the consequences of the Industrial Revolution that swept Europe in the mid-1700s was that more people had more money and more time to spend it in. There was a growing interest in collecting, preserving breeds of animals, and developing new breeds. By the mid 1800s, the tremendous increase in the number of people who kept rabbits resulted in more mutations appearing, and more people interested in becoming involved with these cute creatures for pets.

Clubs were formed to develop colors, patterns, and types. These were displayed at exhibitions. This resulted in the need to draft written standards against which the growing number of breeds could be judged. The rabbit fancy, as an organized hobby, can be said to have developed during the latter part of the 19th century. From then on it just kept growing.

THE GUIDE TO OWNING DWARF RABBITS

In the early years of the 20th century, new breeds were appearing at a tremendous rate. Many looked much the same as other breeds that had been given different names in the same and other countries. As is still the case, if you had something new or different, it would command a higher price if it gained any sort of popularity. As a result, tracing the history of most of today's breeds any earlier than the late 19th century is a minefield of problems.

CHANGES IN THE HOBBY

The breeds that were formerly the most popular tended to be the long-established and large breeds. But as pet and show rabbits gained in popularity, a definite shift toward smaller breeds became evident. The Beveren, Belgian Hare, English and French Lops, Giant Chinchilla, Californian, New Zealand, and their like, all highly popular in the pre-1960s, started to lose ground to the English Spot, the Dutch, the Rex, and other medium-to-small varieties.

THE DEVELOPMENT OF DWARF BREEDS

It is entirely probable that very small rabbits have appeared in litters for many centuries. But these would, at a time when big was most definitely beautiful, be regarded as runts—totally undesirable and of no value. Their litters were small, and they

Dwarf Rabbits, such as Lops, are easier to care for than some of the larger rabbit breeds.

developed a reputation for being sickly.

However, once the rabbit hobby became more organized and shows were clearly going to be a thing of the future, a few breeders started to retain small rabbits and selectively breed them. The first dwarf rabbit that was specifically mentioned in books during the mid-19th century was the Polish, an English breed.

It was regarded at the time as being an unhealthy breed of dubious nature, an unreliable breeder that could not be bred profitably. Even so, some breeders persisted with it. From this breed, all other dwarfs have been produced by hybridization.

Over the years the dwarf breeds have become smaller. During the 19th century, the Polish weighed about three to four pounds. This was considered to be very tiny for a rabbit. Today the same breed must be under two and a half pounds with two pounds being the ideal. It has taken many years to develop other dwarf breeds because many of the die-hard rabbit breeders of the past felt these rabbits were something of a joke. The breeds were not practical.

But enough breeders in Europe could see that small breeds would one day be desirable if the problems associated with dwarfs could be overcome. This has, to a large degree, come to pass. The Netherland Dwarf, more than the Polish, was the breed that really took off during the 1950s. Its success on the show bench projected it to a whole new generation of postwar breeders.

WHY HAVE DWARFS SUCCEEDED?

The most obvious reason why dwarf rabbits have become so popular is because of their size. They require less room and less food. They have been developed in just about every color and pattern seen in rabbits. Pet shops also love them for their small size—it makes them easier to stock. Furthermore, even when adult they still retain a babyish cuteness that pet owners find irresistible.

Another reason the dwarfs are so successful is that, in America in particular, there has been a vast upsurge in the number of pet owners who want to keep their rabbits in their home. The production of many ultra-hygienic indoor cages has in turn made the house rabbit a vastly more acceptable pet than in the past, when wooden cages quickly developed odors from urine.

Dwarfs are popular pets with rabbit owners worldwide.

Choosing a Dwarf Rabbit

Purchasing a dwarf rabbit is not something you should rush into without first giving the matter considerable thought. Unfortunately, many pet owners do not heed this advice. They decide to buy a rabbit on the spur of the moment because the rabbits they have seen in the pet shop are so adorable. Taking any pet into your home should be a commitment for the rest of the pet's life.

This aspect aside, there are many breeds of dwarf rabbits. Some will be more suitable to your needs than will others. If you take all the advice given in this chapter, your chances of purchasing the wrong one will be dramatically reduced—and your chances of obtaining the perfect little pet are more likely.

GENERAL ADVICE

No pet should be purchased specifically for very young children. They soon tire of the pet once the initial novelty has worn thin. Do not expect young children to be responsible for the welfare of a rabbit. Many, though not

Taking a pet into your home requires a lifetime commitment to care. Be sure every member of your household wants and will care for your new pet.

There are many types and breeds of Dwarf Rabbits available to pet owners. Research your options and choose the best rabbit for you.

all, will neglect aspects of day-to-day care. You must be the responsible person, teaching children by your example how to correctly care for their companions.

If the rabbit is to live in the home, it's essential that every member of the household be enthusiastic about this. If not, problems might occur later on if the pet is not managed in the proper manner. This is particularly applicable to routine cleaning of the cage.

Again, in respect to children, understand that dwarf rabbits are much more fragile than their larger cousins. It is imperative that children are taught to handle them gently. Any dogs in the house must be very friendly; otherwise, they might attack the rabbit. These rabbits are very timid and if frightened can bite—or they may go into shock. Consider all of these general points carefully before deciding on a dwarf rabbit.

BREEDING OR SHOW RABBITS?

If you have never owned rabbits before, you may be wanting these cute bunnies for breeding or showing, so a few suggestions may save you a lot of cash and problems. There is no shortage of dwarf rabbits. The first-time owner should forget any stories he may have heard that suggest you can make some extra money as a breeder. The chances of this happening are remote in the extreme.

Even breeding a few litters will generally result in more problems than is justified by the effort and cost.

In general, pet shops are not short of suppliers. There is a world of difference between pet and breeding/show quality. Do not expect any individual dwarf that you purchase at a pet price to produce either quality babies or those capable of winning at shows (other than in pet classes).

If you have aspirations to be a serious breeder or exhibitor, gain experience with one or two pets first. If all goes well and your enthusiasm remains, then is the time to start thinking about obtaining quality stock to breed or exhibit. As you gain practical experience with your pets, you can attend shows and find out much more about that side of the hobby.

PREPARE IN ADVANCE

Once you have decided to own one or more dwarf rabbits, you should obtain their housing and supplies before you purchase the pet. This gives you the time to check out a number of local pet shops to find just the right cage for your needs. With this major item purchased, you have the time to seek out the perfect dwarf rabbit. You then know that you do not need to buy the cage in a rush, possibly not getting quite what you wanted.

With the housing obtained, you can try it in a number of locations to decide where it is best placed in the home for viewing and ease of servicing.

CHOICE OF BREED TYPE

If you want to keep things as simple

Longhaired rabbits, such as the Jersey Wooly, will require more grooming care than a shorthaired rabbit.

as possible, do not select one of the lop-eared or longhaired dwarfs. They are, of course, quite adorable, but long hair requires a lot more attention than does short hair. It can quickly look a mess if not groomed at least once a week.

Be honest with yourself. You know whether or not you or another family member will continue to groom the pet once you have owned it a few weeks. Lop ears are subject to more problems than erect ears—mites, canker, and minor cuts are examples.

HOW MANY AND WHICH SEX?

Rabbits are very social little animals, so you might consider having two rather than one. When the family is not at home, they will be great company for each other. When they are given exercise time out of their cage, you will enjoy watching them play and chase each other around.

If two are purchased, they should be two females (does); two males (bucks), or one of each sex in which one, but ideally both, have been neutered. If two males are kept, both should be of the same young age and also be neutered. Your vet will advise you as to what age your pet should be when he is neutered. Normally, the procedure can be done at about three to four months for a male, a little older for a female.

Neutered pets, especially bucks, are altogether better than those left whole. Males will not have the same sex drives and spraying habits; females will be seasonally less moody. If the pets are desexed, it makes no difference which you choose: either will make a fine pet. Males are possibly a

Rabbits are social animals and you may decide to get more than one. They can keep each other company when you are not home. Be sure to have your pets spayed or neutered.

THE GUIDE TO OWNING DWARF RABBITS

When choosing your rabbit, make sure he is at least eight to twelve weeks old and in good physical condition.

little more bold and adventurous, females more confiding. This is by no means always the case, so you should select the individual that most meets all of your other criteria of color, coat pattern type, and breed.

PURCHASE AGE

Baby rabbits are fully independent of their mother by the age of about eight weeks. Any time after this is a good time at which to obtain a pet. Although some breeders will sell youngsters that are as young as five weeks old, this is not recommended. A rabbit at such an age is far less able to cope with the considerable trauma that is always present when it moves from one home to another.

The stress resulting from this can create many secondary conditions. Stress lowers the performance of the immune system at the very time it is at its lowest point—it is only just beginning to fully develop in the youngster. It is better to play it safe and obtain a baby that has had more time to live an independent life, and those extra three weeks really do make a vast difference to a rabbit.

Indeed, if there are children in your home, a pet of 12 weeks, or older, might be even better because it will be physically stronger. On average, these pets live for about six years, though under ideal conditions they may attain a greater age.

HEALTH IS EVERYTHING

It is vital that a young rabbit is in the peak of health when you obtain it. This cannot be overstressed. So how can you, as a possible first-time rabbit owner, be sure on this account? First, accept that with any young animal nothing is for sure.

Screen the seller by taking note of the conditions under which the rabbits are kept. The accommodations should be spacious and very clean. Water should always be present for the youngsters, and there should be no suggestion that the pets are overcrowded in their housing.

A salesperson who is more interested in selling you a rabbit, whether or not it's a pet suited to your family, is not a good sign. The seller should be able to answer all of your questions—ask them even if you already know the answers.

If you already patronize a given pet store and the staff knows you, this is good. They will be aware that if you are not happy, they could lose all of your pet business. If you do not frequent a given store on a regular basis, be sure to visit all the stores in your locality. You will then have comparisons on which to make a sound judgment.

Choosing your supplier with great care is the best way to ensure that you will obtain a healthy pet. You should also ask if the seller offers a guarantee. More stores are giving these today, but of course they will be limited to a short period. A dwarf rabbit not cared for correctly by its owner can very rapidly deteriorate.

When you inspect a potential pet, it should be lively and able to move around with no signs of limping. The eyes should be round and clear, displaying no indication of weeping. It is absolutely essential that the nose is not discharging liquid. This is an especially worrisome sign in a rabbit.

If the fur on the front feet is wet, this indicates that the rabbit is wiping its eyes and nose a lot—this is a sign of snuffles. The ears should be clean and fresh smelling, with no signs of brown wax or parasites. Check the anal region, which should be clean, showing no staining or congealed fecal matter. The fur should be full of life, with no bald areas, sores, abrasions, or lumps.

You must inspect the teeth. The dwarf breeds, less so the mini rabbits, can suffer from a congenital condition called malocclusion. This is when the upper teeth do not meet, and just overlap, those of the lower jaw. A rabbit's teeth grow throughout its lifetime. If the teeth are not aligned, they will not be worn down by eating and grinding of the jaws. They can grow out of the mouth and curl, or grow into the opposite jaw, creating pain and an inability to eat correctly.

The reason dwarfs are more prone to this problem than are other rabbits

The rabbit you adopt should be clean, alert, and show no signs of illness. Inspect the fur, eyes, teeth, and ears of all potential pets.

Dwarf Rabbits are popular pets with rabbit fanciers worldwide. Be sure to give your rabbit lots of love and provide the best care you can.

is because the structure of their head is modified from normal. This can affect the alignment of the incisors in particular.

COST OF A DWARF OR MINI RABBIT

Dwarf rabbits are no more expensive than their larger cousins but do reflect the general popularity and availability of a given breed. In some rural localities, the less popular varieties will be harder to locate than if you live in a large city. But your pet shop should be able to special order any of the breeds.

The total start-up cost, to include cage, feeders, and food, will be no more than that for a typical purebred puppy or kitten.

Housing a Dwarf Rabbit

Not so many years ago, pet rabbits were considered to be outdoor pets. Most were kept in outbuildings or hutches in the garden. There, any odors from the rabbits, or unsightly hutches, would not prove offensive. Times have changed dramatically. As the hobby has grown, and small rabbits become more popular, the concept of keeping these cute mammals in the home has become very common.

Manufacturers now produce a whole range of housing designed for the "in home" pet, or "house rabbit." These cages are made of materials that make cleaning a simple chore. In the past, most pet rabbit hutches were crudely made of wood. They absorbed urine and gave rabbits a quite unjustified reputation for being smelly.

Rabbits are as fastidious as cats in their personal hygiene. They devote considerable time to washing their fur. If their housing is ever unsightly or odorous, it's either because it is not being cleaned as it should be, is too small, or is not designed to allow for thorough cleaning.

BASIC CONSIDERATIONS

Any rabbit home must provide the pet with somewhere to sleep, eat, attend its toiletry needs, and move around. The hutch should be constructed of materials that can be easily cleaned with no risk that odors will be absorbed into the structure. It should be secure, having no sharp projections that could injure the rabbit. If any exposed wood is incorporated into its structure, it must be protected from being gnawed on by the rabbit.

Cage size will be dictated by the amount of time the pet will be given free-running exercise time. The more time the pet is confined to his little home, the larger the housing must be. However, if a small home is connected to an exercise run, the house need be little more than a place to retreat to and sleep in. Finally, the cage must be located where it's not subjected to sudden changes in temperature or to bright light from which the rabbit cannot retreat.

HOUSING OPTIONS

There are two basic types of rabbit housing. One is the traditional hutch; the other is a cage. For the in-house rabbit, the cage is now by far the most popular choice, as it is for breeders and exhibitors. Wooden cages are still manufactured, largely for outdoor use. They are substantially more expensive than indoor cages because they should be constructed of wood thick enough to withstand changes in the weather. Indoor wooden cages are no longer popular because they are so difficult to keep clean. Most indoor cages today are made of wire or plastic.

WIRE CAGES

Wire cages come in such an array of designs that only the basic components are discussed so that you can be aware of the various options that can be featured in a unit. Visit a number of pet stores to see as many models as you can. Many wire units will require some assembly, but this is very simple and requires only J-clips or regular pliers. Some are assembled by the store, while others are manufactured as assembled units.

Cages can be purchased complete with legs and even small wheels so that they can be moved around—very useful when cleaning the cage area. Some are unfurnished; others will have built-in feeder pots and may include a water bottle. Deluxe wire cages will have a sleeping compartment, complete with a removable or hinged lid.

FLOORING OPTIONS

A rabbit should not be kept on an all-wire bottomed cage, as damage to its feet will occur. You can overcome this by covering the bottom of the cage with a rug, wood, or purchase a cage with a solid plastic bottom.

A recent innovation in cage floors is the use of plastic crossbars wide enough to be comfortable for the rabbit, yet have spaces between them to allow fecal matter to fall through to a tray below. The bars are easily wiped clean.

Access to most cages is via a front-panel door. The roof may also open to give you overhead access, a useful feature for lifting out your rabbit. Be sure the door is large enough to make access very easy for cleaning. In

The Netherland Dwarf is a very popular breed with rabbit fanciers.

If you have more than one rabbit, be sure to provide ample housing for all your pets.

some units, the wire cage is clipped to the base so that you can lift it for thorough cleaning. The wire can be galvanized, chromium plated, or epoxy coated. Chromium will, of course, be very expensive.

Some wire cages are designed as single compartment units; others can be divided to form two cages by the use of solid or wire dividers. They may have double-opening roofs, or front/side panel doors. They are often used as transport cages by exhibitors.

CAGE DIMENSIONS

A bigger cage is always better. The cage should be about four times the size of your rabbit so it can move about the cage freely. There are many cages to choose from and you can even design your own custom cage.

For a single dwarf rabbit kept as a house pet given plenty of time out of its cage, the minimum cage dimensions should be 30x36x18 inches high. The hole size of the wire should be either 1 inches square (2.5cm) or 1x1/2 inches (2.5x1.25cm). The gauge, or thickness, of the metal should be enough so that it does not easily bend.

If two pets are kept together, increase the cage size. Each rabbit should have plenty of space to hop around, even if its taken out of the cage for daily exercise. Cages come in a wide range of dimensions, some being almost square, others being oblong. Cage heights are also very variable but should be high enough so that if the pet raises itself on its hind legs, it still has an inch or two of space above its head.

CAGE FURNISHINGS

The obligatory furnishings are food and water containers, a litter pan, and litter. Optional furnishings are a nestbox and toys of various kinds. The nestbox allows the rabbit to retreat to a darkened area when it wishes to and equates to the natural security of the burrow. Your rabbit will feel safe and secure in the nestbox and will probably spend a lot of time there playing with toys and napping.

Some cages have removable nestboxes fitted to the outside. They are very useful for breeders because they can easily be inspected and cleaned while the doe is eating.

Water is best supplied via a gravity-fed water bottle. It keeps the water free of dust, fecal matter, floor

Rabbits should not be housed on wire-bottomed cages. The rabbit should be supplied with appropriate bedding, a water bottle, and a food dish.

covering, and food. Purchase the best quality bottles: they will not drip like the inexpensive models.

Open dishes are fine in large cages, but they must be heavy; otherwise, the pet will tip them over. They must be cleaned and filled daily. Food can be supplied in a heavy bowl or via special rabbit food containers clipped to the cage wires. You can connect water bottles to your main water system so that the supply lasts longer, but such an arrangement is normally used only by those with many cages and rabbits.

Floor covering can either be fresh aspen or white pine shavings. Do not use cedar shavings: they are dangerous to small animals. The phenol in them can badly affect the respiratory system. Sawdust is too fine and clings to food, as well as to the urogenital organs, where it can create sores.

A nestbox can be any shelter just large enough for the pet to enter and exit with ease. Litter trays are handy for retaining fecal matter. You can also purchase special urine splash deflectors to fit inside the cage. Rabbits are clean animals and most will quickly learn how to use a litter tray.

Rabbit toys can include logs, twigs, and similar items of wood on which to gnaw and throw about. Never supply items made of plastic or rubber. If they are chipped and swallowed, they could prove lethal. Rocks to clamber on and tunnels to explore will be enjoyed, but these are more appropriate for large enclosures because of the space they require.

EXERCISE RUNS

All rabbits should be given the opportunity to exercise every day. It is essential for their physical and mental well-being. An exercise run is the easiest way to make sure your pet can run freely and safely. If you do not have the space for an outside run, you can allow your rabbit free access to a room in your home. Make sure the room is "rabbit-proofed" and that any electrical wires are covered or put out of the rabbit's reach. Rabbits will chew on anything, so keep an eye on your rabbit when it roams freely.

Indoor and outdoor exercise runs are easy to fashion by stapling weldwire onto a wooden frame. An indoor run can have a plastic- or linoleum-covered base so it's easily cleaned. An outdoor run that has a weldwire mesh roof and floor is great for warm days, when it can be placed on the lawn.

It's essential that if a rabbit is left unattended outdoors in a run for any length of time, there should be a shelter section that it can retreat to and avoid direct sunlight when he wishes. This also protects the rabbit from rain. A mesh roof is essential to prevent predators—dogs, cats,

Although Dwarf Rabbits can be left outside (with supervision) to exercise, they should not be kept in outdoor housing. They will enjoy spending time in your home with you.

snakes, or birds of prey—from entering and harming your pet. The run can be moved to different locations and should be used only in good weather. Be sure it is supplied with water and dry food.

LOCATION OF THE CAGE

The main considerations when putting the cage in your home are:

1. It should not be placed where it will be subject to direct sunlight for long periods.

2. Do not place the cage directly over, or adjacent to, a heater unit or air conditioning vent. This will result in temperature fluctuations that can result in dangerous chills, and possibly stress if the rabbit gets too hot or too cold.

3. Avoid placing the cage opposite to outside doors, which will result in drafts and short, rapid temperature changes, especially in the colder months.

4. Place the cage on a raised solid surface, or on legs, so it's at a convenient height for viewing and servicing. If you have cats or dogs in the house, make sure they cannot get into the cage or knock it over.

5. Place the cage where any floor-covering material or foods that fall out of the cage will not create a mess on hard-to-clean surfaces, such as carpets.

The cage should be placed in an active area of your home, so the rabbit can interact with family members. Rabbits are social, friendly creatures and will enjoy lots of attention.

OUTDOOR HOUSING

Dwarf and mini rabbits are not recommended for outdoor hutches unless the climate is mild year round. Even then, the hutch would need to be wooden and very well insulated with a sleeping compartment totally enclosed other than for an access door or hole. A rubber flap over this makes it more cozy on cold windy days.

If dwarfs are placed in a well-constructed outbuilding, such as for breeding units, it is suggested that some form of heating is supplied to ensure that it never gets too cold.

INDOOR BIRD AVIARIES

If space is not a problem and you wish to provide very generous indoor housing for one or more dwarf rabbits, you might consider an indoor aviary. These are modestly priced and offer large floor space for a pet. You can double this by adding a mid-level floor reached by a safe, treaded ramp. Such aviaries are basically constructed the same as rabbit cages but are simply much larger. Your pet shop may stock them, or they can be ordered directly from specialist bird cage suppliers.

Feeding a Dwarf Rabbit

Rabbits are herbivores, which means they live on a diet composed of foods of vegetable origin. They are so easy to feed that sometimes owners supply them with boring diets, forgetting that they like variety. The essential constituents of a rabbit diet should be a blend of numerous foods that ensures nothing important is missing, yet provides for choice and interest.

Hay is an important food item for rabbits, as it provides necessary roughage in their diets. There are many types of hay available, but whichever type you purchase, make sure it's safe for rabbits.

RABBIT PELLETS

Pelleted food should form the staple part of the diet. Pellets contain all the nutrients known to be of importance to the rabbit. They are the most convenient food and have a good shelf life if stored correctly. They do not attract flies, so they have a greater exposure life than other food items once they have been placed into the pet's cage. They also provide something hard on which the rabbit can use to keep his incisor teeth trim.

Do not assume all pellets are the same. Each manufacturer produces its own blend. Purchase the quality brands to ensure the pellet contains the needed amounts of protein, fiber, fats, minerals, and vitamins. Store pellets in a dark, dry cupboard, and keep the bag or box closed to retain freshness. Never feed a pellet that looks moldy, has any sort of foul smell to it, is crumbly, or which may have been fouled by mice or rats—all of these are dangerous.

HAY

This is the most important food item after pellets. It provides vital roughage that helps keep the digestive system moving at the desired pace for good metabolism. It is a food that can be usually supplied on an unrestricted (free choice) basis because it will require a considerable amount to make a pet fat. Hay is any green forage dehydrated such that its moisture content is below 15 percent.

There are many types of hay, such as timothy, bromegrass, orchardgrass, and alfalfa. Those produced from legumes, such as alfalfa, have greater protein content than those cured from grasses. But they are more prone to attack by mold, may become more dusty, and have a greater laxative effect if the pet is not accustomed to them.

From a pet owner's viewpoint, it is sufficient to be aware of these facts. They should purchase only specially prepared hays sold for rabbits and other hay-eating animals. Breeders, who might purchase hay by the bale, are advised to learn more about the different types. Basically, if a hay looks too dusty, or if it shows signs of mold, it should be discarded. Store all hay where it is dry, cool, airy, and protected from rodents.

Hay is especially beneficial to longhaired rabbits because its high fiber content minimizes the risk of hairballs, as well as other gastrointestinal problems.

GRAIN AND SEEDS

Rabbits enjoy any of a wide range of grains and seeds. Mixes containing sunflower, wheat, oats, linseed, soybean, and pellets are sold in all pet shops. Each grain or seed has a different constituent value (protein, carbohydrate, fats, minerals, and

Pellets are the staple of a rabbit's diet, but you must also offer hay and fresh vegetables.

With the proper diet and exercise, your rabbit will live a long, healthy life.

THE GUIDE TO OWNING DWARF RABBITS

Rabbits should be fed grains and seeds as well as fresh fruits and vegetables. Try a few different types to see what your pet prefers.

vitamins) to that of another seed, which is why a mix ensures a more balanced feed.

However, an excess of some grains and seeds can create obesity and digestive upsets, so it is suggested that you keep the quantity small until you have developed a knowledge of their constituent values in respect to protein, carbohydrates, and fats.

PLANTS, FRUITS, AND VEGETABLES

Most greenfoods that you can eat will also be enjoyed by a rabbit. Some examples are apples, carrots, cauliflower, spinach, celery, broccoli, and beans. Wild plants, such as dandelion, plantain, shepherd's purse, wild grasses, and chickweed are favored items.

Pieces of fruit tree branches are excellent for their fiber content and for helping to keep the rabbit's teeth trimmed. Points to remember when feeding any fresh plant food are that it should be fresh, never showing signs of wilting, overripeness, or mold.

All fresh plant foods should be rinsed first to remove any residual chemicals that might be present from crop spraying, especially if they have been gathered from gardens or roadsides. Fresh foods have a limited exposure life. Those not eaten by the rabbit within a few hours should be removed and trashed.

Where flowers and wild plants are concerned, you should work on the basis that unless you are sure they are safe they should not be fed. Books from your library will be useful on this matter, or contact your local or state agricultural department.

TREATS AND SUPPLEMENTS

Sweet candies, cakes, and similar foods have no benefit to a rabbit, so never give them as treats. Instead, offer any of the items discussed, or such foods as baked brown bread, which is good for their teeth. Vitamin and mineral supplements should not be needed by a pet supplied with a balanced diet; they could actually create problems. Supply them only under veterinary advice.

WHEN TO FEED

The actual time when a pet is fed is not as important as the regularity of the time. This means you can determine the time most convenient for you but, having done so, this should be adhered to as much as possible. Ideally, it is best to supply two feeds a day rather than one large one. Rabbits are browsers and prefer a steady intake of food so that their stomach always has a flow passing through it. This is its naturally evolved method of eating. Fresh foods are best supplied in late afternoon/early evening when owners may have more time to spend with their pet. Dry foods can be given in the morning, or you can give a blend of the two types at each feed. The important point is that the day's total ration be apportioned, if possible, between two (or more if this isn't a problem) feeds.

Your rabbit's diet can be supplemented with treats such as alfalfa blocks or squares that are available in your pet store.

HOW MUCH TO FEED

There is no one method for calculating how much food each rabbit should be given per day. Every expert has his own view of this (and of feeding generally) based on his experiences and knowledge of what works for him. Some owners feed on a food-to-body weight basis, others on free-choice methods, yet others on a trial-and-error basis, using fitness as their guide.

The problem of fixed-food quantity to body weight is that quantity is directly influenced by the quality and constituents of the food. Further, some animals need a greater amount of food to maintain a given body weight than others. Also, some pets are a lot more active than others. A more active rabbit will eat more than a rabbit that is less active.

Free-choice methods are very sound in theory but in reality can result in obesity when applied to animals kept in close confinement conditions, which most pets are. The pets are often stressed to a greater or lesser degree. As a consequence, they eat for eating's sake to compensate for boredom, rather than because they need the food.

This leaves the trial-and-error method. This author prefers this method and has used it very successfully over a forty-year period across a range of animals, from rabbits and birds, to hedgehogs and horses. The concept is that a quantity of food is given to the rabbit and the time taken to consume it is noted. If most of the food is eaten quickly, a little more is given.

At the next meal, the extra quantity is supplied and feeding is observed again. If too much is left, the quantity is adjusted at the next meal. The ideal state is when most of the fresh foods are eaten, and a small amount of dry food is left. These will be eaten over the next few hours.

By this method, the desired quantity is soon established. It is then a case of making very minor adjustments based on the individual's state of health and fitness as the months go by.

Feeding is not, and can never be, an exact science. It is a combination of applying known nutritional needs to common sense, and a good deal of observation. A little experimentation can also be a valuable asset to an owner.

AVOIDING FEEDING PROBLEMS

Pet owners can experience health problems as a consequence of not understanding important aspects of feeding principles. For example, scours, an acute diarrhea, can result from eating greenfoods. The problem invariably stems from a situation in which a pet has been reared on dry foods—pellets and grain—and is suddenly given a glut of greenfoods.

A larger or more active rabbit will generally consume more food than a smaller or less active one. Monitor your rabbit to see how much he eats in one day.

Its digestive system cannot cope with such a sudden dietary change: the result is diarrhea. No food item should ever be given in sudden quantity. The chances are it will create digestive problems.

The gut bacteria needed to break down one type of food is different from that required by another food. Also, grain and pellets tend to slow down the digestive process; greenfoods, including hay, speed it up. Rapid changes from one rate to the other is a recipe for problems, just as it would be if you were to suddenly eat a range of foods that your stomach was not accustomed to.

The correct way to feed is to make any changes very gradually and keep the amounts very small. When a pet is first obtained, it's essential the new owner finds out exactly what it has been fed on. This should be maintained for about seven days while the pet settles into its new home and overcomes the trauma of the move. Then, if it is deemed beneficial, its diet can be widened very gradually.

A pet reared on only pellets and grain should be given hay before any greenfoods are introduced. After about two weeks, small amounts of vegetables and greenfoods can be added to the diet. Again, bear in

THE GUIDE TO OWNING DWARF RABBITS

mind that these items are only supplements, not the mainstay of the diet. The digestive system is then able to adjust. Colonies of the gut bacteria needed to break down these new foods will proliferate sufficiently to cope with that particular food type (high in moisture, rich in fiber and vitamins).

Do not allow children to suddenly give their pet a whole apple if it normally never eats these, or usually has a very small piece. The same applies to other items. In the spring when grass is plentiful, it is dangerous to suddenly place a handful in the pet's cage—this sort of feeding causes problems.

COPROPHAGY

As you may be aware, ruminants, such as cows, chew cud. They regurgitate foods from their stomach and eat it again. The food thus gets two passes through the digestive system in order to extract maximum nutrition from it. Rabbits are not ruminants, but they utilize a similar process that enables maximization of foodstuffs. They produce special cecal pellets that are voided at the anus and eaten. These are quite different from fecal pellets. If you were unaware of coprophagy, you might think the rabbit was eating its own fecal matter. For this reason, some rabbit

Be sure to provide your rabbit with fresh food and water each day.

Like people, rabbits can become overweight from eating an excess of food and not exercising. Your rabbit should have daily exercise to keep him in good mental and physical condition.

owners do not like mesh floors because cecal pellets drop through them, thus are lost to the rabbit. This is no cause for concern if the diet is well balanced.

OBESITY

Possibly the most common problem in many pets, including rabbits, is obesity resulting from an excess of the wrong foods relative to the actual energy needs and activity level of the pet. When a rabbit becomes obese, its diet should be scrutinized to reduce high protein and carbohydrate content. Do not attempt to place pets on rapid loss starvation-style diets. This is potentially very dangerous because it may remove the pet's ability to synthesize vital vitamins.

It is better to gradually reduce the quantity of food supplied each day (but over a period) and try to increase exercise time: often this is a good method with pets retained for too long in their cage. High-calorie foods include pellets and certain grains and seeds. If in doubt about dieting, or any nutritional question, consult your veterinarian. This is your safest route.

Dwarf Rabbit General Care

From the moment a pet dwarf rabbit is purchased, his entire quality of life will depend on how his new owner attends all his husbandry needs. Sadly, many owners start with great enthusiasm and good intentions. But, a little bit at a time, the rabbit's care becomes neglected and his freedom restricted. The result is the millions of very sad pets one sees confined to inappropriate housing, unkempt, underfed, and in other ways abused.

Please, do not become such an owner because there are far too many mistreated pets already. Every year thousands of rabbits are abandoned or placed into animal shelters. Many will be destroyed because homes cannot be found for them. The only way this carnage will cease is if each new owner accepts, and lives up to, his full responsibility to the pets he keeps.

It is important for your rabbit's safety to handle him correctly. This is the proper way to lift a rabbit. Never lift rabbits by their ears.

If you handle your rabbit every day, he will become accustomed to being touched and be more social.

COMING HOME

Collect your new pet only after you have his housing and other needs ready. Early in the day is a good time to bring home the bunny so he has all day to become accustomed to his home. Baby rabbits are so cute and friendly that you can handle and pet them once they have had a little time to rest and maybe feed.

If you stop for shopping or a break on a trip, never leave your rabbit in the vehicle on hot days. The rabbit will die from heat stroke. It is not prudent to stop en route to show the new pet to friends. Make the journey home as quickly as possible.

HANDLING RABBITS

It's important that rabbits are handled correctly; otherwise, they will try to wriggle free. If dropped, they may easily be injured. Children can be badly scratched or bitten if they are not taught the right way to handle their new friend.

As a pet owner, it is your responsibility to provide the best care possible to your rabbit for his lifetime. Do all you can to ensure a good quality of life for your pet.

Always approach the bunny so he can see you. Take hold of the loose skin above his shoulders to secure him, then slide your other hand under his body and lift. Once lifted, you can bring the pet to your chest with one hand around his body so he's secure, yet comfortable. Never lift rabbits by their ears. This is painful, harmful to the ears, and will most certainly prompt the pet to wriggle violently.

The important thing about lifting a rabbit is that one hand should provide support for his abdomen and rear end, while the other hand steadies the head and neck. If the underparts are not secured, the pet will rake with his back legs in an effort to gain foot security.

Once the pet is accustomed to being lifted, he will have no fears about it, and variations on lifting and holding can be used. These must always be based on the body weight being supported by the owner's hand. A pet accustomed to being lifted and handled will be a much friendlier companion. It will be easier to groom and more accepting toward regular physical checkups.

HOME AND GARDEN SECURITY

Before a bunny is allowed to run around the house, and certainly the garden, these areas should be checked so they are secure and free of any dangers. In the home, place electrical cables neatly away from the

If you allow your rabbit outside, be sure he does not eat wild flowers that may make him sick or nibble on grass that has been treated with lawn chemicals.

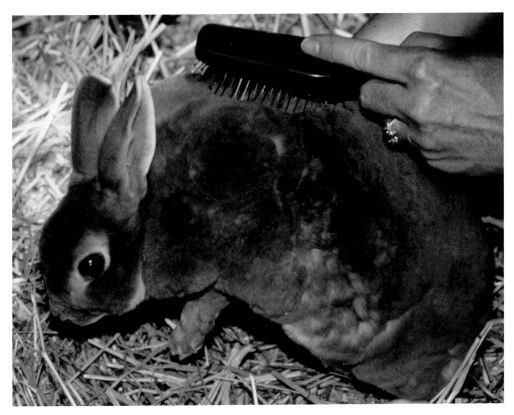

Even though rabbits groom themselves daily, they need to be combed at least once a week. Long-haired breeds will need to be combed twice weekly.

pet's path so there is no chance the rabbit might nibble on a live wire. Keep indoor plants well out of reach of rabbits—some household plants are poisonous to rabbits.

The kitchen is not a good place for a rabbit to be running free when someone is cooking. They could trip over the bunny and spill boiling liquids. Never leave wires from power tools or irons trailing from above when a pet is roaming freely. The rabbit may tug on the wire and bring the tool or iron crashing onto it. Keep cupboard doors closed, especially if they contain dangerous household chemicals.

During warm weather, be sure external doors are not left open, or your pet may decide to go for a walk outside—and it could be the last time you see your cherished little friend. Also, be aware that drafts may slam a door shut on your pet: guard against this possibility by using a heavy door stop. Keep rabbits away from open windows as well.

If the pet is given garden playtime, be sure he is always under adult supervision, unless he's in a secure exercise run. If left by himself, he might start to eat flowers or vegetables which may have been treated with toxic chemicals. The

Rabbits are clean and neat pets. They can even be trained to use a litter box like a cat.

rabbit may wander beyond, or dig under, a fence and get lost. Dogs and cats will chase and may kill an escaped dwarf rabbit if they get the chance.

Rabbits are very curious little animals, and, being reared as pets, they are not as aware of dangers as are their wild cousins. Their owner must at all times think of their safety as they would for a human toddler.

GROOMING

Rabbits are like cats in that they continually groom themselves. However, regardless of whether they are shorthaired or longhaired, they need grooming on a regular basis. The shorthaired breeds can be attended to once a week—or more if you enjoy doing it.

Longhaired breeds should be groomed at least twice a week. Use a medium-stiff bristle brush for shorthaired rabbits and the same, plus a comb, for longhaired rabbits.

If snags are present in a long coat, never pull on them, as this will upset the pet. Gently tease them apart with your fingers.

Be very gentle when using a comb because it is easy to apply too much pressure. This will make the grooming process unpleasant for the rabbit, especially on his more delicate underparts.

Grooming should encompass regular checking of the teeth, ears, and nails. If the incisor teeth display any misalignment, have your vet trim them before they cause problems. Teeth inspection and care is crucial to a rabbit. Any signs of mites or brown-black wax in a pet's ears should be treated by the vet.

THE GUIDE TO OWNING DWARF RABBITS

Superficial wax on the ear flap can be routinely wiped away using a cleanser from your vet, or with a dampened swab. Never probe into a rabbit's ears because this could cause considerable damage.

The nails should not require undue attention if the pet is given adequate exercise time. However, the very tips may need periodic trimming using clippers sold for dogs and cats. Be careful never to trim too much or the "quick" may be cut. This is the blood and nerve supply seen as a pink area in the nail. If in doubt, let your vet attend to this and then show you how to do it.

Rabbits should not be bathed unless it is absolutely essential—such as for severe parasitic invasion. They can easily become chilled. Generally, clean, fresh bedding, coupled with regular grooming, is sufficient to keep the coat in sparkling and fresh smelling condition. The occasional use of a dry shampoo from your pet store should suffice to remove any dirt or stains that might be found in the coat.

Cornstarch or chalk powder will also act as a dry shampoo. But they must be thoroughly brushed from the coat after use to avoid the risk the pet will ingest them continually as he licks his fur. If a bath is necessary, be very sure the rabbit is kept in a warm room for 24 hours afterward. Dampness, in any form, can be dangerous to a pet rabbit.

OTHER PETS

Although some rabbits do become friends with dogs and cats, it is always wise to supervise free house roaming rabbits when other pets are in residence. Dogs in particular can easily

Never leave a rabbit outside unsupervised unless he is in an outdoor run or exercise cage. Do all you can to keep your pet safe.

kill a rabbit in a moment of overexcited play. Ferrets are natural enemies of a rabbit, and cats may try to catch a small dwarf rabbit.

CONTROLLING ODORS

Rabbits are not odorous. If any smells emanate from their housing, it's because the cage is not being kept clean enough. Modern cages are easy to wipe clean and do not absorb noxious smells. The source of odors is the ammonia and its compounds present in urine and fecal matter. Housing should be cleaned every day, or at least once a week, and fresh bedding supplied with similar regularity.

Food should not be allowed to remain in the cage to sour. Apart from contributing to odors, the bacteria that colonize it can quickly gain access to the pet's internal organs. When cleaning the cage, be sure to clean the cage bars. Rabbits often rub their snouts on them and can ingest parasites and pathogens (disease-causing organisms).

LITTER TRAY TRAINING

When a pet is first allowed free exercise in a home, he should be restricted to one room. A litter tray should be placed in a convenient spot for the pet to use. It can contain a biodegradable clumping litter—not the silicon clay types that can be dangerous to the pet's respiratory and other systems.

Once the pet is seen to use the tray on a regular basis, another room can be made open to it, and the procedure repeated. If a pet starts to foul the carpet, or eliminate behind chairs, the area must be cleaned with an odor neutralizer. Ideally, do not let the pet use that room again until all traces of odor have been removed from carpets with a biological odor neutralizer. Litter training a rabbit can be done to a relatively high degree of success if enough patience is used and litter trays are placed in strategic positions in rooms where the pet is allowed to exercise.

Health Care for Your Dwarf Rabbit

The key to keeping a dwarf rabbit healthy is by paying particular attention to day-to-day hygiene, good feeding, and ensuring the pet is well exercised so it does not become bored and subject to stress factors. An owner should also be able to spot the signs of ill health and react quickly to them. Clearly, the more rabbits, or even other pets, that are kept in the same environment, the greater the chances things can go wrong—the more so if standards of general care should start to fall.

GENERAL HYGIENE

Neglecting simple hygiene can become the cause of major problems.

The following is a useful checklist of chores that should be done on a regular basis and should not be neglected.

Clean food and water dishes daily and gravity-fed water bottles at least every other day. Replace any that become chipped or cracked.

Completely strip down and clean each cage once a week—more often if the cage is obviously in need of it. Never leave soiled flooring material in the vicinity of the cage—trash it as soon as possible. Remove uneaten food before it has time to sour.

In very hot weather, when flies are prevalent, place a piece of mesh over the pet's cage to restrict these pests from the rabbit's housing. Store all foods in dry, cool, well-ventilated cupboards, ensuring they are not at risk to contamination by mice, rats, or beetles. Thaw all frozen foods, and never refeed foods already fed, but uneaten, by the rabbit.

Always wash your hands before and after handling your pets, especially if any of them are ill or suspected of being so. Do likewise

A dedicated rabbit owner should be able to spot any signs of ill health and react quickly to them. Good husbandry practices will keep your rabbit in the best of health.

after gardening. Millions of pathogens live in soil, or alight on it, and can easily be transferred to house pets by direct handling or during food preparation.

STRESS

After hygiene, stress is probably the singular most important source of illness. It has special significance to dwarf rabbits, which are timid and more susceptible to stress than the larger breeds. It depresses the correct functioning of the immune system and affects the nervous system. Its consequences may be displayed in a number of ways.

The pet becomes prone to illnesses that ordinarily would not be a problem. A minor chill can develop into a major illness, or recovery from an illness becomes complicated by secondary conditions related to an ineffective immune system.

The pet may develop syndromes. These include the eating of fecal matter as opposed to the normal cecal pellets, self-mutilation, pacing, overgrooming, trichophagia (hair eating), hyperphagia (overeating), and polydipsia (insatiable thirst).

The rabbit shows aggression, or its opposite, nervous immobility (dyskinesia).

Stress can affect a rabbit's breeding ability, and a doe's ability to correctly rear her babies—if she will even attempt to do this. Abandonment and cannibalism are often stress-induced problems.

Stress may affect one pet more than another because it is acting on a genetic background that is better in some rabbit lines than others for temperament. A further complication of stress is that many of its identifiable expressions may be the result of other irregularities that have a definite metabolic, rather than mental, source.

However, when any health or behavioral problem is observed, it is wise to consider stress as the prime, or a contributing, factor. Routinely consider the possible sources of this. They are: overcrowding, incorrect diet, lack of space, lack of exercise, uncleanliness in the pet's housing, fluctuating temperatures, excessive disturbance when resting, excessive incorrect handling, bullying by another rabbit or pet, and fear derived from regular, but sudden, noises (vacuums, machinery, and their like). Moving the rabbit's home and regular transportation (in some show rabbits) are also stressors.

QUARANTINE

For breeders and exhibitors, the need to quarantine stock is vital to reduce the risk of introducing health

Stressful conditions such as overcrowding, excessive disturbance, and loud noises can lower a rabbit's immune system. Keep a close eye on your rabbit, if you think he is stressed, do what you can to make him feel more secure.

A healthy rabbit will appear alert and bright-eyed. If you think your pet is ill, do not try to diagnose the problem yourself, contact a vet.

THE GUIDE TO OWNING DWARF RABBITS

problems. In a well-managed stud, an area away from the main stock will be prepared to isolate all incoming stock. A separate area will also be made for hospitalizing unwell rabbits. Newly acquired stock and returning exhibition individuals should be isolated for 14-21 days in order to ensure they are not incubating diseases or problems contracted just before they arrived into the breeder's rabbitry.

RECOGNIZING HEALTH PROBLEMS

The more involved you are with your pet, the more rapidly you will recognize the first signs of ill health. These will be displayed in the rabbit's behavior, and via physical signs.

Behavioral signs are: eating and drinking more or less than usual; disinterest in your approach when it is normally excited; lethargic movements and excessive sleeping; retreating to a dark corner; displaying obvious distress when lifted or handled; erratic movements not typical of its behavior patterns; rapid breathing; and disinterest in favored treats.

All of these are cause for concern and a more careful observation, or a physical examination of the rabbit. Sometimes the signs are normal. For example, after bursts of playful activity a pet will breathe more rapidly, and on hot days it may subsequently eat or drink more than normal. It may get very tired and sleep a little more. Allowance must be made for such situations.

Rabbits mask their pain very well, and some diseases may not show themselves by physical signs. A changed behavior pattern may be the only indication your pet is unwell. For other problems, more typically, changed behavior may be the first sign that precedes physical signs.

Physical signs are: liquid discharge from the nose or eyes; wheezy, labored breathing; sneezing; coughing; muscular contortions; any inflammation on the body, genitals, or nose; lumps; sores (especially on hocks); bald patches; general loss of fur; skin color change; foul body odor; scabs on face or genitals; diarrhea; blood-streaked urine; constipation; potbellied appearance; excessive scratching; loss of weight; failure to gain weight; loss of coordination; and excessive salivation (slobbering). Any physical signs that are not normal for your pet should be investigated.

Odd fecal matter and colored urine may not be problematic, as they may reflect the diet. Certain foods, such as beets, will affect the color of a rabbit's feces.

REACTING TO POSSIBLE ILL HEALTH

The moment you suspect a pet is ill, it should be isolated to a warm, well-

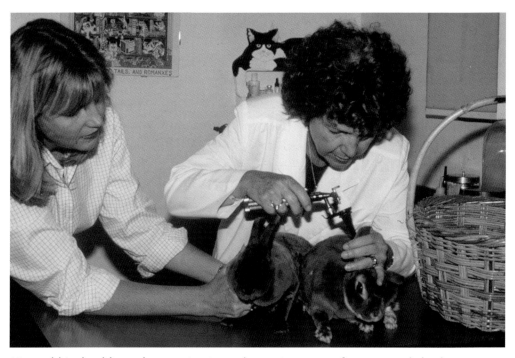
Your rabbit should see the veterinarian at least once a year for a general checkup.

ventilated, and somewhat dimly lit location. The date and time should be noted, along with the reasons you suspected something was amiss. The severity of the signs should dictate your next course of action. If the signs are minor, or rather vague, you might wait for 12-24 hours to see if things return to normal.

If they do not, you should contact your vet immediately, relating the current situation. If possible, gather a number of fecal samples and place them in a small plastic container. If they need to be retained a few hours, put them in the refrigerator, never the freezer. Some recent urine-stained floor covering might also be gathered.

DON'T TRY TO BE A VET

It can be dangerous, even fatal, to attempt home diagnosis based on reading veterinary texts or listening to so-called experts. Some breeders are indeed very well informed on problems, but you cannot be sure the one you talk to is. In any case, veterinary knowledge is always improving, and only a vet will have up- to-date information across a wide spectrum of problems.

Apart from the possible need to do microscopy on blood, fecal matter, or skin scrapings, a treatment cannot be prescribed until the problem is identified. If the amateur gets it wrong, not only is time lost, but any treatment given may be ineffective, or positively dangerous.

If a vet cannot be contacted immediately, all fresh foods should be withheld, **except** for hay and water, plus a few rabbit food pellets, especially if diarrhea is displayed.

Increase the environmental temperature a few degrees, but be sure ventilation is adequate to prevent heat stress becoming a factor.

MINOR WOUNDS AND SHOCK

Small cuts and abrasions will generally heal rapidly. Bathe the area in tepid water and apply a non-stinging antiseptic liquid or cream. More serious wounds should be lightly bandaged over a swab to stem the blood flow, then the pet should be rushed to the nearest vet.

If a rabbit is attacked by a cat or dog, or is otherwise in shock—displayed by collapsing, eyes not focusing or "staring," it should be placed in a warm, quiet, dark location to recover. It is better that it should be given a veterinary check over: a drug may be recommended to overcome any side effects.

THE FIRST AID CHEST

It is always prudent to have a first aid chest in the home, especially if your vet is some distance away or in case he or she cannot be contacted when needed. Suggested contents should include: flat-pointed, curved, blunt-ended scissors; cotton balls and swabs; various-sized bandages; styptic pencil or similar coagulant; antiseptic and antibiotic lotions; eye lotion; iodine; a stomach emulsion for minor upsets; thermometer, and treatments for fleas, mites, and worms.

AFTER AN ILLNESS

It is essential, especially for those with numerous rabbits and/or other pets, that during and after an illness husbandry techniques should be carefully reviewed to prevent the possibility that problems will recur. All cages should be stripped and thoroughly cleansed using a dilute bleach solution. Rinse with clean water and allow to dry before the pet is put back into his home.

If a rabbit dies without displaying physical signs, a postmortem is beneficial. Most aspects of preventive medicine require only your work effort and diligence. Yet they can make the difference between never having a major problem to deal with, and the loss of one or more cherished pets.

A final comment is that a routine visit to your vet at least once a year is strongly recommended. At such time the vet can check the nails, teeth, and ears as well as all other bodily parts. Any corrective treatment or suggestions may prevent future problems, worry, and expensive treatments.

Exhibition of Your Dwarf Rabbit

RABBIT EXHIBITIONS

Without rabbit shows, there would be no rabbit-fancy hobby, nor all of the many breeds today kept as pets, which include all the dwarf and mini rabbits. At no other event can you view so many different rabbit breeds in their many colors and patterns. For a breeder, the show is the final judgment of their years of effort and investment.

As a beginner, you can meet top exhibitor/breeders. At the large

Valuable rabbits, such as show-quality rabbits, are often tattooed for identification purposes.

shows, the breed clubs have booths, while manufacturers display their latest products. The show is the shop window to the entire hobby. Shows range in size from small and informal to major national shows attracting thousands of exhibits from every area of your country. Visitors come to these large shows from all over the world looking to buy from the best stock your nation's breeders produce.

CLASSES AND STANDARDS

There are usually two types of classes held at shows. By far the most important and numerous are those for registered stock of given breeds. But classes for pets are often featured to encourage pet owners to taste the flavor of the exhibition side of the hobby.

The main show classes are for each breed and the colors in them. There are classes for bucks and does, as well as junior and senior classes—these

Rabbit shows judge breeds based on a written set of standards and all show-quality rabbits must be of excellent type, color, and coat. If you are interested in showing rabbits, attend a few exhibitions in your local area.

encompassing both the exhibitor and the rabbits themselves. Junior, or youth, exhibitors in America are under 19 years of age, in Britain under 16. In the dwarf breeds, a senior buck or doe is over six months old, a junior under six months on the day of the show.

The breeds are judged against written standards of excellence drafted for each breed. Class winners progress to meet other class winners of the same breed until a best of breed is established. The breed class winners move on to compete against the other breeds' winners (bucks and does), and by this process a Best in Show and Best Opposite Sex are finally proclaimed—a great honor for the winning breeders.

Each country organizes its shows and classes in their own manner, but the essentials follow the broad system outlined.

Clearly, a show rabbit must be of excellent type, color, and coat. It must be in the peak of fitness. A minor lack of color or a seemingly small fault that would be of no consequence to a pet will be enough to keep a show rabbit from the top awards in a major show, though it still might be a winner or place exhibit at a smaller, more local event.

An exhibitor must devote considerable time to preparing a rabbit for a show, especially in the longhaired breeds. It is definitely an area of the hobby that is only for the really enthusiastic owner.

Any rabbit lover is advised to attend at least one or two shows so they can see the range and quality of show stock. If they become enthused, they can join the nearest club, as well as their national governing body—the American Rabbit Breeders Association in the US, and the British Rabbit Council in the UK.

Dwarf & Mini Breeds

Before discussing the breeds, it is of interest to establish a few points with respect to the rabbits generally held to be members of a group regarded as dwarf and mini. These are relative terms not having any official definition. The dwarf and mini rabbits are those derived by crossings involving the Netherland Dwarf or any other breed that is a dwarf or mini.

With the exception of the Mini Rex, all dwarfs and minis have very characteristic head shapes and a small ear size. Most have a weight of under four pounds, the Mini and Dwarf Lops, plus the Mini Rex, being the three exceptions.

Smallness in the dwarf breeds is not the result of a single gene mutation, as in color, so it cannot be expressed in a genetic formula. It is the result of polygenic action in which quantitative genes for smallness are present. If a dwarf or mini breed is mated to a larger rabbit, the offspring will range in size between the extremes of the parents.

If any of the offspring are paired back to the dwarf parent, a similar range of sizes will be apparent, thus establishing that dwarfism is neither a dominant nor recessive mutation. However, when a rabbit carries the required number of genes for smallness, anatomical changes take place in head structure. These produce the characteristic dome shape associated with these breeds, and the smaller ear size. Also, the foreshortening of the jaw creates the potential for malocclusion of the teeth.

As might be expected in such small rabbits, dwarfism is coupled with smaller litter size. However, infertility

There are many breeds of Dwarf Rabbits to choose from. They vary in size and weight. This Holland Lop generally weighs less than four pounds.

is an associated problem. Breeders must distinguish between small numbers and very small litter size created by partial infertility. There is also a link between dwarfism and suspect temperament, so one way or another the dwarf breeds should not be casually bred. They are suited only to those who are prepared to cull whenever needed in order to continually remove any that display the negative traits associated with extreme smallness.

It should be mentioned that there is a recessive mutant gene for dwarfism in rabbits that results in offspring death before or at birth. This is not found in the general rabbit-fancy population at this time.

Although we tend to think dwarf and mini breeds are very small, it should be remembered that this appears to be the case only because we are comparing them with most other domestic rabbits, which, historically, were bred for largeness. Wild rabbits are often no more than three or four pounds in weight.

In theory, it is possible to develop a dwarf or mini variety of any current rabbit breed, but the reality may not be quite so simple. Size is also influenced by modifying genes. Its effect in one breed can be different to that in another.

It is thus a very complex area of the rabbit fancy best left to experts who are prepared to devote years of experimental breeding to produce new varieties. These will arrive, given the present popularity of all adorable little bunnies.

For the purposes of this chapter, the following breeds are regarded as dwarf rabbits or mini rabbits: Netherland Dwarf, Britannia Petite (Polish in Britain), Dwarf Hotot, Polish (American), Jersey Wooly, Holland Lop, American Fuzzy Lop, Mini Rex, Dwarf Lop, and Mini Lop. They are discussed on the basis of weight, the lightest first. The weights quoted are the upper limits for exhibition individuals, but the ideal may be somewhat lighter. In pet examples, the upper weight is sometimes exceeded, especially in the lops that have a stocky build.

NETHERLAND DWARF

This is a very popular rabbit in the rabbit fancy of the western countries. It should weigh no more than two pounds and have short, erect ears under two inches. The origins of the breed are obscure. It is thought to have been developed from the Polish breed of Britain, so it is the second

The Netherland Dwarf is short and compact, with deep-set shoulders.

oldest of the dwarfs. The white Polish was exported to Europe around the mid-19th century, where it became the European Polish. The German version of the Polish was crossed with the Dutch, itself a developing breed at the time, to create the Hermelin. This, and others like it, possibly including some wild rabbits, resulted in a stable size.

The European Polish was developed in Europe under a range of names and colors and was exported from Holland to Britain around 1948. It was named the Netherland Dwarf because Britain already had a Polish: the original white Polish. The Netherland was crossed with many other breeds in Britain to add new colors. It arrived in America during the 1950s but did not gain official recognition until 1969.

In its early development, the Netherland Dwarf had a bad reputation for being aggressive,

A Dwarf Hotot is an attractive, all white rabbit with a circle of black around its eyes. They reach a maximum weight of three pounds.

The Polish (American) rabbit is comparable to the Netherland Dwarf and is becoming quite popular.

highly nervous, prone to dental problems, and difficult to breed. But over the years, careful breeding programs have reduced these problems, and the Netherland has become the archetypal dwarf used to develop the other dwarf and mini breeds.

This rabbit is the personification of cute and charming. It is available in just about every color and combination of colors that can be had in rabbits, plus the pointed pattern known as Himalayan. Because there are so many backyard breeders of this popular dwarf, selection for good health, temperament, and dental work are priorities.

BRITANNIA PETITE

This is the original dwarf breed. It is said to have appeared in England as an albino in a litter of an unspecified breed. It was originally called a Polish. Why it was named Polish seems to have been lost in time. This breed made its way to mainland Europe,

where it became very popular. The Netherland Dwarf evolved from it. Its arrival in the US, under the name Polish, created problems because it was crossed with the Netherland and much confusion arose.

Eventually, the breed that is known as the Polish in Britain was called the Britannia Petite in the US. However, while the Polish of Britain is seen in as many colors as the Netherland Dwarf, the Britannia Petite of the US has only two varieties: red-eyed white and black otter. It is not recognized in Britain. Its maximum weight and ear length are the same as for the Netherland Dwarf. The ears should touch along their length, as in the Polish, whereas in the Netherland Dwarf this need not be so.

DWARF HOTOT

This very attractive little dwarf cannot be confused with any other rabbit at this time. It's all white, but it has a circle of black hair around its eyes, giving it a very distinctive and pleasing appearance. The Dwarf Hotot's maximum weight is three pounds with an ear length not exceeding three inches. It was developed during the 1970s in both East and West Germany. The breeds involved were the Hotot (Blanc de Hotot in Britain), a French breed, red-eyed white rabbits, and a black Netherland Dwarf. It arrived in the US in 1981 and gained official recognition in 1983. It is a breed that has gained a steady and growing following in the US and has devotees in Britain as well.

Interestingly, a breed called the Husumer existed in Germany in the early part of this century. It was similar to the Hotot but had a black tail as well as black eye rings. Maybe the Dwarf Hotot will be used to develop such a variety as a new dwarf, such is the potential for these small rabbits.

POLISH (AMERICAN)

The breed known as the Polish in the US is somewhat different from its British counterpart, which is called the Britannia Petite in the US. It is seen in fewer colors and is heavier,

being up to three pounds, with an ear length to three inches. In stature, it is comparable to the Netherland Dwarf. Its color range is black, blue, chocolate, and white.

It has become steadily more popular over recent years and is a good choice for those looking to get started in a breed with a future, yet is not so popular that established competition is overwhelming. As a pet, it is less readily available than the Netherland Dwarf.

JERSEY WOOLY

If you like a longhaired rabbit and are prepared to devote enough time to its coat, the Jersey Wooly could be the answer. Its weight limit is three and one half pounds, the ear length is

Jersey Woolys are popular long-haired rabbits and are seen in a wide range of colors. They were introduced into the rabbit hobby in 1988.

a maximum of three inches. The profuse coat with a hair length of two to three inches gives it a larger appearance than its actual body size. It was developed during the 1970s by Bonnie Seeley of New Jersey, who used a number of breeds to create it. Official recognition came in 1988.

The Jersey Wooly has gained tremendous popularity in a short span of time as an exhibition rabbit and is seen in a wide range of colors. One of the Jersey's great attributes as a pet is that it has a very gentle temperament, which no doubt has helped its popularity. It may sport tufts of hair on its ears, but they must not form heavy tassels as seen in the larger English Angora breed.

HOLLAND LOP

The lightest of the dwarf and mini lops, the Holland Lop should weigh no more than four pounds, with pendulous ears hanging to one inch below the jaw when held in a natural position. In fact, this breed can raise

Holland Lops are one of the most popular Dwarf Rabbit breeds today. They are friendly and adorable pets.

its ears so that they are held at an angle from the body, sometimes even semi-erect.

Its origins go back to the breeder Adrien De Cock of Holland, who started trying to develop a dwarf French Lop. It was to be a long series of matings that included the French and English Lops, plus the ubiquitous Netherland Dwarf.

After much hard work, the result was the Netherland Dwarf Lop. This became the Holland Lop in the US after its introduction in 1976, and official recognition in 1986.

Today, the breed is the most popular dwarf breed after the Netherland. Its heavy build and gorgeous expression, coupled with a delightful temperament, have catapulted it to popularity in under a decade and gained it a reputation as a huggable dwarf. It is available in many colors and patterns. Its pendulous ears should be regularly inspected for good health, but this apart, it is an easily managed breed.

AMERICAN FUZZY LOP

The second of the longhaired dwarfs, the Fuzzy Lop is best regarded as a Holland Lop with long hair. Body weight should not exceed four pounds. While the ears should hang to the same depth as the Holland, they start higher on the head. They are covered with fur, not wool, as on the body. The wooly hair

The American Fuzzy Lop is a popular long-haired breed developed from crosses between the Holland Lop and the Angora.

length is secondary to density, which should be even all over the body.

The breed was developed from crosses between the Holland Lop and Angora to improve coat type. These crosses occasionally produced longhaired Hollands. These were paired together and eventually became the Fuzzy Lop, which gained recognition in 1988.

Available in a wide range of colors and patterns, the American Fuzzy is a great breed for those who enjoy grooming and appreciate nice wool on their pets. Very popular as a show dwarf, the breed makes a delightful pet with a very nice nature. Consider carefully that extra grooming is essential with this breed.

MINI REX

Unusual in this group of diminutive bunnies, the Mini Rex does not display the typical dwarf head shape. Instead, it is a true mini of its parent breed, the Rex. The upper weight limit is four and one quarter pounds in the US, and four pounds in Britain. The ears are erect—longer than erect-eared dwarfs, but in a nice ratio to the head and body size.

The breed was officially recognized in the US in 1988 after careful

The Mini Rex is available in a wide range of colors and has a velvet-like coat of fur. A Mini Rex would make a beautiful pet for any rabbit fancier.

sponsorship and development by Mona Berryhill of Texas, and other breed devotees. It was not originally a planned breed but was developed after a very small individual was found in a litter of normal Rex rabbits. This was paired to a Netherland Dwarf, and the concept of a diminutive Rex was underway.

The main feature of this breed, as with its larger cousin, is a velvet-like coat of fur that wins admirers the moment they first touch it. Add to this the fact that it is available in a wide range of colors, and you have a recipe for a real winner, which the Mini Rex has proved to be. It makes both an outstanding exhibition rabbit and a gorgeous pet. It popularity just keeps on growing.

DWARF LOP

Not recognized in the US, the Dwarf Lop of Britain should weigh no more than five pounds and have ears stemming from the crown in the style of the larger French Lop, which it resembles in its conformation. It was developed around 1964 in Holland, but the breeds used, other than the French Lop, are not well documented. It is said that the Dutch was one of them.

It arrived in Britain during the late 1960s from Holland, where Adrien De Cock is credited to have been its originator. Some examples were exported to the US, and confusion arose between this breed and the Mini Lop, both being regarded as the same breed on both sides of the Atlantic during the early years.

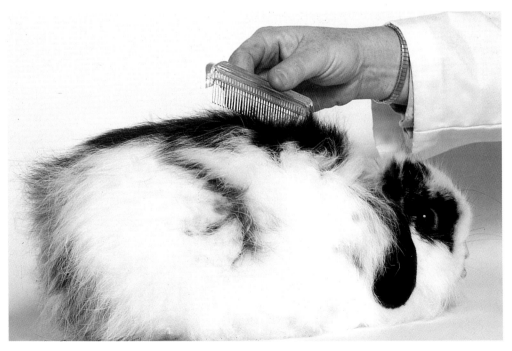

American Fuzzy Lops require a lot of extra grooming if they are to be kept in the best of condition.

THE GUIDE TO OWNING DWARF RABBITS

Mini Lops are popular rabbits that can weigh up to six pounds. They are the heaviest of all the dwarf and mini breeds.

However, today it is accepted that they are in fact quite apart in their actual lineage, even if they share some common ancestry in the breeds used to create them. The Dwarf Lop is seen in a wide range of colors and makes a very lovable pet.

MINI LOP

The heaviest of the dwarf and mini breeds, this rabbit can weigh up to six pounds. Its ears are large and typically French Lop in type, as is its heavy conformation. It originated in Germany as the Kleine Widder. It was first exhibited in the US in 1974, when it failed to gain any great attention. A few breeders persevered with it, and, as small breeds gained in popularity, the breed was renamed the Mini Lop and given official recognition.

It is now a very popular breed. The original US examples were of the agouti (ticked) pattern, and white. Selective breeding using the French Lop and Chinchilla vastly increased the range of colors to those now available. As with all lops, it should have a wonderful temperament. It is more active than its heavier French cousin.

Index

Photo Credits

Joan Balzarini: pp. 31, 41, 50
Isabelle Francais: pp. 7, 8, 11, 13, 14, 18, 21, 23, 29, 30, 32, 35-38, 42, 43, 48, 53, 55-63
Michael Gilroy: pp. 1, 3, 4, 12, 15, 22, 25, 27, 34, 39, 40, 46, 47
Moishe Kopoina: p. 52
R. Pearcy: pp. 5, 9, 17